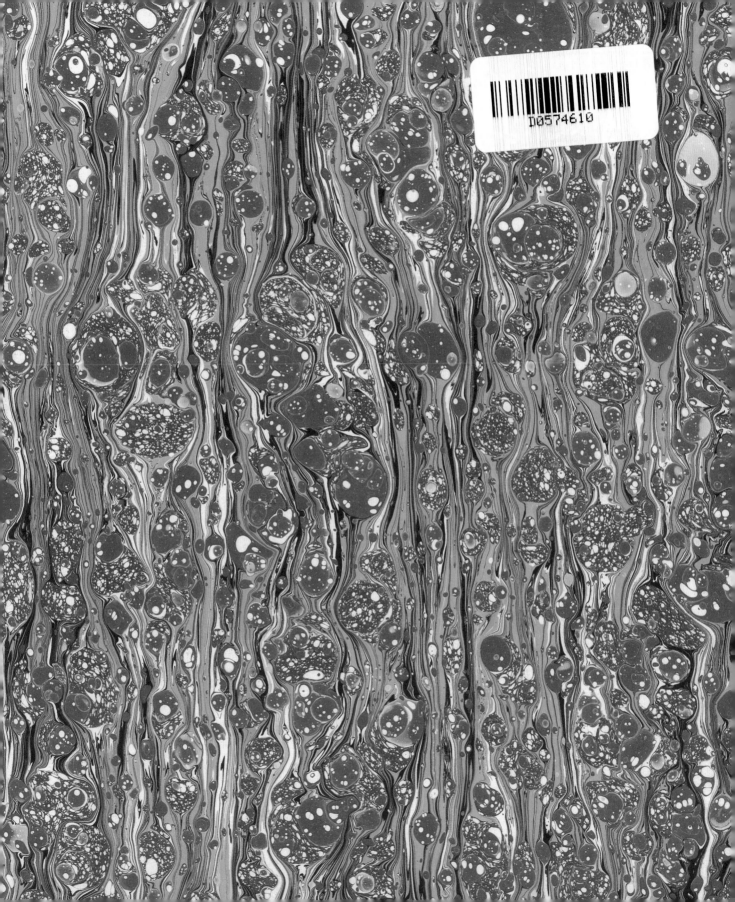

SPRINGS OF JOY

All my springs

are in Thee.
Psalm 87. 7.

Springs of Joy

A Biblical Treasury

Scribed and Illustrated by Evelyn Scaramanga
Translations selected by John Eddison

Crossroad, New York

1995

The Crossroad Publishing Company
370, Lexington Avenue, New York, NY 10017

This edition c Evelyn Scaramanga 1995

First published in the United Kingdom by
Shepheard-Walwyn (Publishers) Ltd, London, 1995

Printed and bound in Singapore by SNP Printing Pte ltd

Library of Congress Catalog Card No: 95-067966

ISBN 0-8245-1502-1

Acknowledgements

We would like to thank all those who at different times and in various ways contributed helpfully towards this book.

Grateful acknowledgement is made to the copyrightholders for permission to include extracts from the translations of the Bible listed below:

Authorized Version of the Bible (King James Bible), the rights of which are vested in the Crown, reproduced by permission of the Crown's Patentee, Cambridge University Press;

New English Bible © Oxford University Press and Cambridge University Press 1961, 1970;

Revised English Bible © Oxford University and Cambridge University Press 1989;

New International Version, Hodder and Stoughton Publishers UK and Zondervan Publishing House, USA;

Revised Standard Version © 1946, 1952, 1971 by the Division of Christian Education of the National Council of Churches of Christ in the USA;

Good News Bible published by The Bible Societies/ Harper Collins Publishers Ltd, UK © American Bible Society, 1966, 1971, 1992;

J.B. Phillips © Harper Collins Publishers Ltd.

For permission to quote from 'God's Plan for Man', page 13, by Finis Jennings Dake, grateful acknowledgement is made to Dake Bible Sales Inc. P.o. Box 1050 Lawrenceville, Georgia 30246 USA

Dedicated

To the treasured memory

Of my beloved husband

George Ambrose Scaramanga

In whose prayer and thought

This Book

Had its earliest beginnings

Contents

Acknowledgements

Preface

Springs of Life   1

Springs of Faith   17

Springs of Love   33

Springs of Peace   49

Springs of Praise   65

Springs of Comfort   81

Springs of Fellowship   97

Springs of Encouragement   113

Springs of Hope   129

Prayer   145

Abbreviations   147

Index   148

Preface
The Bible

The Bible is God's inspired revelation of the origin and destiny of all things. It is the power of God unto eternal salvation and it is the source of present help for body, soul and spirit. It is God's will and testament to men in all ages, revealing the plan of God for man here and now and in the next life. It contains God's message of salvation to all who believe in Christ, and of eternal damnation to those who rebel against the Gospel. It is the Book that contains the mind of God, the state of man, the way of salvation, the doom of sinners and the happiness of believers. Its doctrines are holy, its precepts binding, its histories true and its decisions immutable. Read it to be wise, believe it to be safe and practice it to be holy. It contains light to direct you, food to support you and comfort to cheer you. It is the traveller's map, the pilgrim's staff, the pilot's compass, the soldier's sword and the Christian's charter. Here Heaven is opened and the gates of hell disclosed. Christ is its grand subject, our good its design and the glory of God its end. It should fill your memory, rule your heart and guide your feet in righteousness and true holiness. Read it slowly, frequently, prayerfully, meditatively, searchingly, devotionally and study it constantly, perseveringly and industriously. Read it through and through until it becomes part of your being. It is a mine of wealth, the source of health and a world of pleasure. It is given to you in this life, will be opened at the judgment and will last forever. It involves the highest responsibility, will reward the least to the greatest labour and will condemn all who trifle with its sacred contents.

From 'God's Plan for Man'
Finis Jennings Dake

Springs

of

Life

HEAR A FATHER'S

INSTRUCTION

Be attentive, that you may gain insight
    For I give you good precepts:
Do not forsake my teaching.
    Incline your ear to my sayings
Let them not escape from your sight
    Keep them within your heart.
For they are life to him who finds them
    And healing to all his flesh.
Keep your heart with all vigilance
    For from it flow the Springs of Life.

Proverbs 4.1, 20-23. R.S.V.

I AM THE WAY, THE TRUTH AND THE LIFE.

No man cometh unto the Father but by Me.

He that believeth on the Son hath everlasting life: and he that believeth not the Son shall not see life. And this is the record, that God hath given to us eternal life, and this life is in His Son. He that hath the Son hath life, and He that hath not the Son of God hath not life.

John 14.6; 3.36. 1 John 5.11-12. A.V.

He was in the world but the world, though it owed its being to Him, did not recognise Him. His own would not receive Him, but to all who did receive Him, to those who have yielded Him their allegiance, He gave the right to become children of God, not born of any human stock, but the offspring of God Himself. So the Word became flesh; He came to dwell among us, and we saw His glory, such glory as befits the Father's only Son, full of grace and truth.

1 John 1. 10-14. N.E.B.

4

And this is the testimony

That God gave us eternal life, and this life is in His Son.

He who has the Son has life; he who has not the Son of God has not life.

I write this to you who believe in the name of the Son of God, that you may know that you have eternal life.

And we know that the Son of God has come and has given us understanding, to know Him that is true.

1 John 5. 11-13, 20. R.S.V.

5

I CAME THAT THEY MAY HAVE LIFE.

I am the Good Shepherd. The Good Shepherd lays down His life for the sheep. My sheep hear My voice and know them, and they follow Me; and I give them eternal life, and they shall never perish, and no one shall snatch them out of My hand. My Father, who has given them to Me is greater than all and no one is able to snatch them out of the Father's hand.

John 10.10-11; 27-30. R.S.V.

JESUS
SAID
FATHER, THE
TIME HAS COME

Glorify your Son, that your Son may glorify you. For you granted Him authority over all people that He might give eternal life to all those you have given Him. Now this is life eternal; that they may know you, the only true God, and Jesus Christ, whom you have sent.

John 17. 1-3. N.I.V.

When the Kindness and Generosity Of God our Saviour dawned upon the world, then not for any good deeds of our own, but because He was merciful, He saved us through the water of rebirth and the renewing power of the Holy Spirit. For He sent down the Spirit upon us plentifully through Jesus Christ, our Saviour, so that justified by His grace, we might in hope become heirs to eternal life. These are words you may trust.

Titus 3.5-8. N.E.B.

FOR GOD SO

LOVED THE WORLD

That He gave His one and only Son,
that whoever believes in Him shall not
perish but have eternal life. For God
did not send His Son into the world to
condemn the world, but to save the world
through Him.
Whoever believes in Him is not condemned, but whoever does not believe stands
condemned already because he has not
believed in the name of God's one and
only Son.   John 3.16-18. N.I.V.

When you were slaves of sin

You were free from the control of righteousness; and what was the gain? Nothing but what now makes you ashamed, for the end of that is death. But now, freed from the commands of sin, and bound to the service of God, your gains are such as make for holiness, and the end is eternal life. For sin pays a wage and the wage is death, but God gives freely, and His gift is eternal life in union with Christ Jesus our Lord.

Romans 6. 20-23. N.E.B.

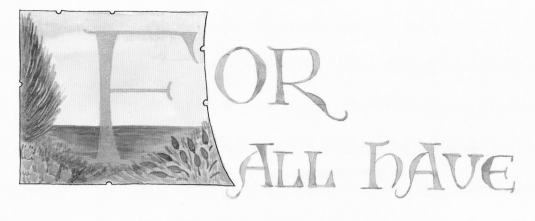

FOR ALL HAVE SINNED

And fall short of the glory of God and are justified freely by His grace through the redemption that came by Christ Jesus. God presented Him as as a sacrifice of atonement, through faith in His blood. He did this to demonstrate His justice, because in His forbearance He had left the sins committed beforehand unpunished. He did it to demonstate His justice, the One who justifies those who have faith in Jesus.

Romans 3. 23-26. N.I.V.

I TELL you the TRUTH, WHOEVER

hears My word and believes in Him who sent Me has eternal life and will not be condemned; he has crossed over from death to life. For as the Father has life in Himself so He has granted the Son to have life in Himself. I am the resurrection and the life. He who believes in Me will live even though he dies. Neither is there salvation in any other for there is none other name under heaven given among men, whereby we must be saved.

John 5. 24; 11. 25. N.I.V. Acts 4. 12. A.V.

YOU DILIGENTLY STUDY THE SCRIPTURES

Because you think that by them you possess eternal life. These are the scriptures that testify about Me, yet you refuse to come to Me to have life. Who ever believes in Me, as the scripture has said, streams of living water will flow from within him. By this He meant the Spirit, whom those who believed in Him were later to receive.

John 5. 39-40; 7. 38-39. N.I.V.

Sir you have nothing to draw

With and the well is deep. Jesus answered, Everyone who drinks this water will be thirsty again, but whoever drinks the water I give him will never thirst. Indeed, the water I give him will become in him a spring of water welling up to eternal life.

To him who is thirsty I will give to drink without cost from the spring of the water of life. He who overcomes will inherit all this. John 14. 11-14. Revelation 21.6-7. N.I.V.

HE SHOWED ME THE RIVER OF THE

Water of Life, sparkling like crystal, flowing from the throne of God and of the Lamb. On either side of the river stood a tree of life. The leaves of the trees serve for the healing of the nations. The throne of God and of the Lamb will be there, and His servants shall worship Him they shall see Him face to face and bear His name on their foreheads. There shall be no more night, for the Lord God will give them light.   Revelation 22. 1-5. N.E.B.

Springs of Faith

 LESSED
IS the
man who trusts
in the Lord,

Whose confidence is in Him,
He will be like a tree planted by the water,
That sends out its roots by the stream.
It does not fear when heat comes,
Its leaves are always green.
It has no worries in a year of drought
And never fails to bear fruit.

Jeremiah 17. 7-8.   N.I.V.

I TELL YOU THE TRUTH.

IF ANYONE SAYS

To this mountain, go throw yourself into the sea, and does not doubt in his heart but believes that what he says will happen it will be done for him.

Therefore I tell you, whatever you ask for in prayer, believe that you have received it and it will be yours, and when you stand praying, if you hold anything against anyone, forgive him so that your Father in heaven may forgive you your sins.

Mark 11. 22-24. N.I.V.

Think of the WILD FLOWERS

They neither work nor weave. Yet I tell you that Solomon in all his glory was never arrayed like one of these. If God so clothes the grass, which flowers in the field today and is burnt in the stove tomorrow is He not much more likely to clothe you, you little-faiths. You must not live in a state of anxiety, your Father knows well enough that you need such things. No, set your heart on His kingdom.

Luke 12.27-28,31. J.B.P.

HEREFORE SINCE WE HAVE BEEN

Justified through faith, we have peace with God through our Lord Jesus Christ, through whom we have gained access by faith into this grace in which we now stand. And we rejoice in the hope of the glory of God. Not only so but we also rejoice in our sufferings, because we know that suffering produces perseverance, perseverance character; and character hope. And hope does not disappoint us because God has poured out His love into our hearts.

Romans 5. 1-5. N.I.V.

FOR I RESOLVED TO KNOW NOTHING WHILE I WAS WITH

You except Jesus Christ and Him crucified. I came to you in weakness and fear and with much trembling.

My message and my preaching were not with wise and persuasive words but with a demonstration of the Spirit's power so that your faith might not rest on men's wisdom, but on God's power.

1 Corinthians 2.2-5. N.I.V.

FAITH COMETH BY HEARING AND

Hearing by the Word of God. Whosoever shall call upon the name of the Lord shall be saved. Now then shall they call on Him in whom they have not believed? And how shall they believe in Him of whom they have not heard? And how shall they hear without a preacher? And how shall they preach except they be sent? How beautiful are the feet of them that preach the gospel of peace. Romans 10.17. 13-15. A.V.

FOR IT IS BY GOD'S GRACE THAT YOU

Have been saved through faith. It is not the result of your own efforts, but God's gift, so that no one can boast about it.

God has made us what we are, and in our union with Christ Jesus, He has created us for a life of good deeds, which He has already prepared for us to do. Now in union with Christ Jesus, you who used to be far away have been brought near by the sacrificial death of Christ.

Ephesians 2.8-13. G.N.B.

WE HAVE
A GREAT
PRIEST IN CHARGE
OF THE HOUSE OF

God. So let us come near to God with
a sincere heart and a sure faith, with
hearts that have been purified from a
guilty conscience and with bodies washed
with clean water.
Let us hold on firmly to the hope we
profess, because we can trust God to keep
His promise.   Hebrews 10. 21-23. G.N.B.

NOW FAITH IS BEING SURE OF

What we hope for and certain of what we do not see. By faith Enoch was taken from this life, so that he did not experience death; he could not be found because God had taken him away. For before he was taken, he was commended as one who pleased God. And without faith it is impossible to please God, because anyone who comes to Him must believe that He exists and that He rewards those who earnestly seek Him.

Hebrews 11. 1. 5-6. N.I.V.

LET US KEEP OUR EYES FIXED ON JESUS

On whom our faith depends from beginning to end. He did not give up because of the cross. On the contrary, because of the joy that was waiting for Him, He thought nothing of the disgrace of dying on the cross and He is now seated at the right hand side of God's throne. Who His own self bare our sins in His own body on the tree. He hath made Him to be sin for us who knew no sin, that we might be made the righteousness of God in Him.

Heb. 12.2. G.N.B. 1 Peter 2.24. 2 Cor. 5.21. A.V.

Is Any one of you sick? he should

Call the elders of the church to pray over him and anoint him with oil in the name of the Lord, and the prayer offered in faith will make the sick person well; the Lord will raise him up. If he has sinned, he will be forgiven.

Therefore confess your sins to each other and pray for each other so that you may be healed. The prayer of a righteous man is powerful and effective.

James 5. 14-16   N.I.V.

THIS IS CAUSE FOR GREAT JOY, EVEN

Though now you smart for a little while if need be, under trials of many kinds. Even gold passes through the assayers fire, and more precious than perishable gold is faith that has stood the test. These trials come so that your faith may prove itself worthy of all praise, glory and honour when Jesus Christ is revealed. Trusting in Him, you reap the harvest of your faith, that is salvation for your souls. 1 Peter 1·6·9. N.E.B.

HE HAS GIVEN US HIS VERY GREAT

And precious promises so that through them you may participate in the divine nature and escape the corruption in the world by evil desires.

For this very reason, make every effort to add to your faith goodness, and to goodness knowledge; and to knowledge self control; and to self control perseverance; and to perseverance godliness; and to godliness brotherly kindness, and to brotherly kindness love.

2 Peter 1·4-7.   N.I.V.

FOR EVERYONE BORN OF GOD

Overcomes the world. This is the victory that has overcome the world, even our faith. This is the confidence we have in approaching God, that if we ask any thing according to His will, He hears us. And if we know that He hears us what ever we ask, we know that we have what we asked of Him. For everyone who asks receives; he who seeks finds, and to him who knocks, the door will be opened.

1 John 5. 4; 14.   Luke 11.10.   N.I.V.

Springs
of
Love

DEAR

FRIENDS,

LET US LOVE

One another, because love comes from God. Whoever loves is a child of God and knows God. Whoever does not love does not know God, for God is love. And God showed His love for us by sending His only Son into the world so that we might have life through Him. This is what love is, it is not that we have loved God, but that He loved us and sent His Son to be the means by which our sins are forgiven.

1 John 4.7. G.N.B.

34

I HAVE
LOVED
YOU WITH AN
EVERLASTING LOVE.

I have drawn you with lovingkindness.
I will build you up again, and you
will be rebuilt.
Again you will take up your tambourines and go out to dance with the
joyful. Now great is the love the Father
has lavished on us, that we should be
called children of God! And that
is what we are! Jeremiah 31.3. 1John 3.1. N.I.V.

If you make the Most High

Your dwelling, then no harm will befall you, for he will command his angels concerning you to guard you in all your ways. Because he loves me, says the Lord, I will rescue him, for he acknowledges my name. He will call upon me and I will answer him. I will be with him in trouble.

I will deliver him and honour him. With long life will I satisfy him and show him my salvation.

Psalm 91,9-11; 14-16. N.I.V.

I WILL MENTION THE LOVING

Kindnesses of the Lord, and the praises of the Lord, according to all that the Lord hath bestowed on us and the great goodness according to His mercies and according to the multitude of His lovingkindnesses.

In all their affliction He was afflicted and the angel of His Presence saved them; in His love and in His pity He redeemed them and carried them all the days of old.

Isaiah 63. 7-9. A.V.

THIS IS MY FATHER'S GLORY

That you may bear fruit in plenty and so be My disciples. As the Father has loved me so have I loved you. Dwell in My love. If you heed My commandments you will dwell in My love, as I have heeded My Father's commandments and dwell in His love. I have thus spoken to you so that My joy may be in you and your joy complete. This is My commandment: love one another as I have loved you.

John 15. 8-13. N.E.B.

THERE IS NO GREATER LOVE THAN THIS

That a man should lay down his life for his friends. You are My friends if you do what I command you. I have called you friends because I have disclosed to you everything that I heard from My Father.

You did not choose Me, I chose you. I appointed you to go on and bear fruit, fruit that shall last; so that My Father may give you all that you ask in My name. Love one another.

John 15. 13-17. N.E.B.

Thus We have come to know and Believe the love which God has for us. God is love; he who dwells in love is dwelling in God and God in him. This for us is the perfection of love, to have confidence on the day of judgement, and this we can have because even in this world, we are as he is. There is no room for fear in love, perfect love banishes fear. We love because he first loved us. But if a man says 'I love God' while hating his brother, he is a liar.

1 John 4. 16-21. N.E.B.

My BROTHERS

DO NOT BE

Surprised if the world hates you. We for our part have crossed over from death to life; this we know because we love our brothers. The man who does not love is still in the realm of death.

It is by this that we know what love is, that Christ laid down His life for us and we in our turn are bound to lay down our lives for our brothers.

You will recognise them by the fruit they bear.

1 John 3.13-16. Matthew 7.16. N.E.B.

Love must be completely

Sincere. Hate what is evil, hold on to what is good. Love one another warmly as Christian brothers and be eager to show respect for one another. Work hard and do not be lazy. Serve the Lord with a heart full of devotion. Let your hope keep you joyful, be patient in your troubles and pray at all times. Share your belongings with your needy fellow Christians and open your homes to strangers.

Romans 12.9-13. G.N.B.

AND THIS IS MY PRAYER THAT YOUR

Love may grow ever richer in knowledge and insight of every kind, enabling you to learn by experience what things really matter. Then on the day of Christ you will be flawless and without blame, yielding the full harvest of righteousness that comes through Jesus Christ to the glory of God. If then our life in Christ yields any consolation of love, any participation in the Spirit, fill up my cup of happiness with the same love.

Philippians 1.9; 2.1-2. R.E.B.

I PRAY THAT OUT OF HIS GLORIOUS RICHES HE may strengthen you with power through **HIS SPIRIT** in your inner being so that **CHRIST** may dwell in your hearts by faith, and **I** pray that you, being rooted and established in love, may have power, together with all the saints, to grasp how wide and long and high and deep is the love of **CHRIST**, and to know this love which surpasses knowledge that you may be filled to the measure of all the fulness of **GOD**.

Ephesians 3. 16-19. N.I.V.

Who shall separate us from the love

Of Christ? Shall trouble or hardship or persecution or famine or nakedness or danger or sword? No, in all these things we are more than conquerors through Him who loved us. For I am convinced that neither death nor life, neither angels nor demons, neither the present nor the future, nor any powers, neither height nor depth, nor anything else in all creation will be able to separate us from the love of God that is in Christ Jesus our Lord.

Romans 8. 35, 37-39. N.I.V.

I MAY SPEAK

With the tongues of men and of angels but if I have no Love I am a noisy gong or a clanging cymbal; I may prophesy, fathom all mysteries and secret lore, I may have such absolute faith that I can move hills from their place, but if I have no love I count for nothing; I may distribute all I possess in charity, I may give up my body to be burned, but if I have no Love I make nothing of it. Love is very patient, very kind. Love knows no jealousy; Love makes no parade, gives itself no airs, is never rude, never selfish, never irritated, never resentful; Love is never glad when others go wrong, Love is gladdened by goodness, always slow to expose, always eager to believe the best, always hopeful, always patient. Love never disappears. As for prophesying, it will be superseded, as for tongues, they will cease; as for knowledge, it will be superseded. For we only know bit by bit, and we only prophesy bit by bit, but when the perfect comes, the imperfect will be superseded. When I was a child, I talked like a child, I argued like a child, now that I am a man, I am done with childish ways.

At present we only see the baffling reflections in a mirror, but then it will be face to face, at present I am learning bit by bit, but then I shall understand as all along I have myself been understood. Thus Faith and Hope and Love last on, these three, but the greatest of all is Love.

1 Corinthians 13.1-13. Moffatt.

Springs of Peace

Thou wilt keep him

in perfect peace

Whose mind is stayed on Thee, because he trusteth in Thee.
Trust ye in the Lord for ever, for in the Lord Jehovah is everlasting strength. Lord, Thou wilt ordain peace for us for Thou also hast wrought all our works in us.
Great peace have they who love your law, and nothing can make them stumble.
May the God of hope fill you with all joy and peace as you trust in Him.

Is. 26. 3-4, 12 A.V. Psalm 119. 165 N.I.V. Romans 15.13. N.I.V.

THE LORD BLESS YOU AND KEEP YOU.

The Lord make His face shine upon you
    And be gracious to you;
The Lord turn His face toward you,
    And give you peace.
Let the light of your face shine upon us
    Oh Lord.
I will lie down and sleep in peace
    For you alone, oh Lord
Make me dwell in safety.
    Mercy and truth are met together;
Righteousness and peace have kissed each other.

Num. 6. 24-26. Ps. 4. 6-8. N.I.V. Ps. 85.10. A.V.

TO BE SPIRITUALLY MINDED IS LIFE

And peace. Once more God will send us His Spirit. The waste land will become fertile and fields will produce rich crops. Everywhere in the land righteousness and justice will be done. Because everyone will do what is right, there will be peace and security for ever. God's people will be free from worries, and their homes peaceful and safe. God has called us to peace.

Rom. 8.6. A.V. Is. 32.15-18 G.N.B. 1 Cor. 7.15. A.V.

OR YE SHALL GO OUT WITH JOY AND BE LED FORTH

With peace: the mountains and the hills shall break forth before you into singing, and all the trees of the field shall clap their hands.

Instead of the thorn shall come up the fir tree, and instead of the briar shall come up the myrtle tree; and it shall be to the Lord for a name, for an everlasting sign that shall not be cut off.

Isaiah 55. 12-15. A.V.

How

BEAUTIFUL

on the mountains

Are the feet of those who bring good
news, who proclaim peace, who bring
good tidings, who proclaim salvation, who
say to Zion 'Your God reigns.'
The Lord will lay bare His holy arm
in the sight of all the nations, and all
the ends of the earth will see the salvation
of our God.
For the Lord will go before you, the God
of Israel will be your rearguard.

Isaiah 52. 7,10,12. N.I.V

Though the mountains be

Shaken and the hills be removed, yet My unfailing love for you will not be shaken, nor My covenant of peace be removed. All your sons will be taught by the Lord and great will be your children's peace.

No weapon forged against you will prevail, and you will refute every tongue that accuses you.

This is the heritage of the servants of the Lord.

Isaiah 54. 10, 13, 17. N.I.V.

FIND REST
oh my soul
in God Alone,

My hope comes from Him,
He alone is my salvation,
He is my fortress.
My salvation and my honour depend on God.
He is my mighty rock, my refuge.
Trust in Him at all times,
Pour out your heart to Him,
For God is our refuge.
You, oh God are strong,
You, oh God are loving.

Psalm 62. 5-12. N.I.V.

HE THAT DWELLETH

IN THE SECRET

Place of the Most High shall abide under the shadow of the Almighty. I will say of the Lord, He is my refuge and my fortress, my God, in Him will I trust. Because he hath set his love upon Me, therefore will I deliver him. I will set him on high because he hath known My name. He shall call upon Me and I will answer him. I will be with him in trouble. I will deliver him and honour him.

Psalm 91. 1-2; 14-16. A.V.

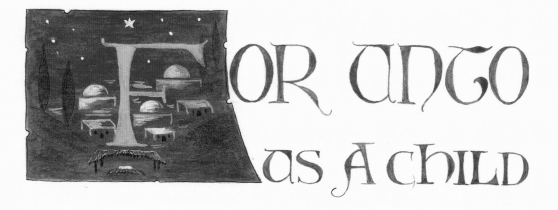

OR UNTO
US A CHILD
IS BORN, UNTO US
A Son is given, and the government
shall be upon His shoulder: and His name
shall be called Wonderful Counsellor,
the Mighty God, the Everlasting Father,
the Prince of Peace.
Of the increase of His government and
peace there shall be no end, upon the throne
of David, and upon his kingdom to order
it, and to establish it with judgment and
with justice from henceforth even for ever.

Isaiah 9.6-7. A.V.

THIS IS WHAT THE LORD SAYS

I am the Lord your God, who teaches you what is best for you, who directs you in the way you should go. If only you had paid attention to My commands, your peace would have been like a river, your righteousness like the waves of the sea. They did not thirst when He led them: He made water flow for them from the rock. 'There is no peace', says the Lord, 'for the wicked.'

Isaiah 48.17-18; 21-22. N.I.V.

COME UNTO ME ALL YE THAT LABOUR

And are heavy laden, and I will give you rest. Take My yoke upon you and learn of Me: for I am meek and lowly in heart; and ye shall find rest unto your souls. For My yoke is easy and My burden is light.

Matthew 11. 28 -30. A.V.

PEACE IS MY PARTING GIFT TO YOU.

My own peace, such as the world cannot give. Set your troubled hearts at rest and banish your fears. The hour is coming, has indeed already come, when you are all to be scattered, leaving Me alone. Yet I am not alone, because the Father is with Me. I have told you all this so that in Me you may find peace. In the world you will have trouble. But courage! The victory is Mine. I have overcome the world.

John 14.27, 1; 16.31-33. N.E.B.

BE CAREFUL FOR NOTHING

BUT IN EVERYTHING

By prayer and supplication with thanks giving, let your requests be made known unto God.

And the peace of God which passeth all understanding shall keep your hearts and minds through Christ Jesus.

Now the Lord of peace Himself give you peace always by all means.

Let the peace of God rule in your hearts.   Phil. 4. 6-7. 2 Thes. 3. 16. Col. 3. 15. A.V.

LET THE PEACE OF CHRIST RULE IN

Your hearts and be thankful. Let the word of Christ dwell in you richly as you teach and admonish one another with all wisdom, and as you sing psalms, hymns and spiritual songs with gratitude in your hearts to God.

And whatever you do, whether in word or deed, do it all in the name of the Lord Jesus, giving thanks to God the Father through Him. Peace I leave with you; My peace I give you.

Colossians 3. 15-17. N.I.V.

Springs of Praise

PRAISE the LORD.

PRAISE GOD

In His sanctuary.
Praise Him in His mighty heavens,
    Praise Him for His acts of power,
Praise Him for His surpassing greatness,
    Praise Him with the harp and lyre,
Praise Him with tambourine and dancing,
    Praise Him with the strings and flute,
Praise Him with the clash of cymbals,
    Praise Him with resounding cymbals
Let everything that has breath
    Praise the Lord.

Psalm 150.1-6. N.I.V.

I WILL EXTOL THE LORD AT ALL TIMES.

His praise will always be on my lips.
Glorify the Lord with me
Let us exalt His name together.
I sought the Lord, and He answered me,
He delivered me from all my fears.
Those who look to Him are radiant.
The angel of the Lord
Encamps around those who fear Him,
And He delivers them.
For those who fear Him lack nothing.
The Lord is close to the brokenhearted.

Psalm 34.1, 3-5, 7, 9, 18. N.I.V.

YOU ARE my GOD,

EARNESTLY I SEEK YOU

I have seen you in the sanctuary
And beheld your power and your glory.
Because your love is better than life
My lips will glorify you.
I will praise you as long as I live.
With singing lips my mouth will praise you,
On my bed I remember you,
I think of you through the watches of the night.
Because you are my help
I sing in the shadow of your wings.
Your right hand upholds me.

Psalm 63. 1-8. N.I.V.

I WILL EXALT YOU

my GOD the KING.

Every day I will praise you.
Great is the Lord and most worthy of praise,
His greatness no one can fathom
I will meditate on your wonderful works
They will celebrate your abundant goodness.
The Lord is faithful to all His promises
And loving towards all He has made.
The Lord is near to all who call on Him
He fulfils the desires of those who fear Him
He hears their cry and saves them,
Let every creature praise His holy name.

Psalm 145. 1-3, 5, 13, 18, 19, 21. N.I.V.

PRAISE
BE TO THE
GOD AND FATHER

Of our Lord Jesus Christ who has blessed us in the heavenly realms with every spiritual blessing in Christ. For He chose us in Him before the creation of the world to be holy and blameless in His sight. In love He predestined us to be adopted as His sons through Jesus Christ, in accordance with His pleasure and will, to the praise of His glorious grace which He has freely given us in the One He loves.

Ephesians 1.3-6. N.I.V.

PRAISE the LORD.

HOW GOOD IT IS

To sing praises to our God
   How pleasant and fitting to praise Him.
He heals the broken hearted
   And binds up their wounds.
Great is our Lord and mighty in power,
   His understanding has no limit.
Sing to the Lord with thanksgiving,
   Make music to our God on the harp.
The Lord delights in those who fear Him,
   Who put their hope in His unfailing
Praise the Lord.   love.

Psalm 147. 1,3,5,7,11,20. N.I.V.

As for me I shall Always have hope

I will praise you more and more,
Your righteousness reaches to the skies.
Oh God, you who have done great things,
Who oh God is like you?
Though you have made me see troubles
Many and bitter,
You will restore my life again
And comfort me once again.
I will praise you with the harp,
For your faithfulness, oh my God
My lips will shout for joy.

Psalm 71.14, 19-23. N.I.V.

But you
are a
chosen people,

A royal priesthood, a holy nation, a people belonging to **G**od, that you may declare the praises of **H**im who called you out of darkness into **H**is wonderful light. **O**nce you were not a people, but now you are the people of **G**od, once you had not received mercy, but now you have received mercy. **L**ive such good lives among the pagans that though they accuse you of doing wrong, they may see your good deeds and glorify **G**od.

1 Peter 2.9-12. N.I.V.

Shout with joy to God,

Let the sound of His praise be heard.
He has preserved our lives
And kept our feet from slipping,
For you, oh God, tested us,
You refined us like silver.
We went through fire and water
But you brought us to a place of abundance.
God has surely listened,
Praise be to God
Who has not rejected my prayer
Or withheld His love from me.

Psalm 66. 1, 9, 10, 12, 19, 20. N.I.V.

74

AWESOME

IS THE

LORD MOST HIGH,

The great King over all the earth!
He chose our inheritance for us.
Sing praises to God, sing praises,
Sing praises to our King, sing praises,
For God is the King of all the earth.
Sing to Him a psalm of praise.
God is seated on His holy throne -
The nobles of the nations assemble
For the kings of the earth
Belong to God;
He is greatly exalted.

Psalm 47. 2,4,6-9. N.I.V.

75

BLESS the LORD

oh my SOUL

And all that is within me
Bless His holy Name.
Bless the Lord, oh my soul
And forget not all His benefits,
Who forgiveth all thine iniquities,
Who healeth all thy diseases,
Who redeemeth thy life from destruction,
Who crowneth thee with lovingkindness
And tender mercies,
So that thy youth is renewed
Like the eagles. Bless ye the Lord.

Psalm 103. 1-5, 21.   A.V.

Through Jesus

Therefore Let

Us continually offer to God a sacrifice of praise, the fruit of lips that confess His name. And do not forget to do good and to share with others, for with such sacrifices God is pleased. May the God of peace, who through the blood of the eternal covenant brought back from the dead our Lord Jesus, that great Shepherd of the sheep, equip you with everything good for doing His will and may He work in us what is pleasing to Him.

Hebrews 13. 15, 20. N.I.V.

As I Looked I Heard the Voices

Of many angels, thousands on thousands, myriads on myriads. They proclaimed with loud voices:

Worthy is the Lamb who was slain to receive power and wealth, wisdom and might, honour and glory and praise.

Then I heard all created things crying Praise and honour, glory and might to Him who sits on the throne and to the Lamb for ever. The elders prostrated themselves in worship.

Revelation 5. 11-14. R.E.B.

78

Oh the Depth
of the Riches

Of the wisdom
    And knowledge of God!
How unsearchable are His judgments
    And His paths beyond tracing out!
Who has known the mind of the Lord
    Or who has been His counsellor?
Who has ever given to God
    That God should repay him?
For from Him and through Him
    And to Him are all things
To Him be the glory for ever. Amen.

Romans 11. 33-36. N.I.V.

Springs of Comfort

COMFORT
YE, COMFORT
YE MY PEOPLE,
Saith your God. He shall feed His flock like
a shepherd. He shall gather the lambs in
His bosom, and shall gently lead those that
are with young. Who hath measured the
waters in the hollow of His hand and meted
out heaven with the span and comprehended
the dust of the earth in a measure, and
weighed the mountains in scales.
Who hath directed the Spirit of the
Lord or being His counsellor hath taught
Him? With whom took He counsel?

Isaiah 40. 1, 11-14. A.V.

HUMBLE YOUR

SELVES THEREFORE

Under the mighty hand of God, that in due time He may exalt you.
Cast all your anxieties on Him for He cares about you.
And after you have suffered a little while, the God of all grace who has called you to His eternal glory in Christ, will Himself restore, establish and strengthen you.
To Him be the dominion for ever and ever. Amen.

1 Peter 5. 6, 10. R.S.V.

Since Then we have a great High Priest

Who has passed through the heavens Jesus, the Son of God, let us hold fast our confession. For we have not a High Priest who is unable to sympathise with our weaknesses, but who in every respect has been tempted as we are, yet without sin.

Let us then with confidence draw near to the Throne of Grace that we may receive mercy and find grace to help in time of need.

Hebrews 4. 14-16. R.S.V.

WITH EVERLASTING KINDNESS WILL I

Have mercy on thee, saith the Lord, thy redeemer. For the mountains shall depart and the hills be removed, but My kindness shall not depart from thee, neither shall the covenant of My peace be removed. With great mercies will I gather thee. O thou afflicted, tossed with tempest and not comforted, behold I will lay thy stones with fair colours and lay thy foundations with sapphires, all thy borders of pleasant stones.

Isaiah 54.8, 7, 10-12. A.V.

The Redeemed of the Lord

Shall return and everlasting joy shall be upon their head; and they shall obtain gladness and joy; and sorrow and mourning shall flee away. I, even I am He that comforteth you; who art thou that thou shouldest be afraid of a man that shall die and forgettest the Lord, thy Maker that hath stretched forth the heavens and laid the foundations of the earth. I have covered thee in the shadow of Mine hand.

Isaiah 51. 11-13, 16. A.V.

86

FOR ALL those

WORDS WHICH WERE

Written long ago are meant to teach us today; that when we read in the scriptures of the endurance of men and of all the help that God gave them in those days. we may be encouraged in our own time. May the God who inspires men to endure. and gives them a Father's care give you a mind united towards one another. You will sing from the heart the praises of God the Father, so open your hearts to one another.

Romans 15. 4-7. J.B.P.

87

PRAISE BE TO THE FATHER

And the God of all comfort who comforts us in all our troubles so that we can comfort those in any trouble with the comfort we ourselves have received from God. For just as the sufferings of Christ flow over into our lives, so also through Christ our comfort overflows. If we are comforted it is for your comfort which produces in you patient endurance of the same sufferings we suffer; so also you share in our comfort.

2 Corinthians 1.3-7. N.I.V.

THE SPIRIT OF THE LORD GOD IS UPON ME

Because the Lord hath anointed Me to preach good tidings unto the meek. He hath sent Me to bind up the broken hearted and to proclaim liberty to the captives, and the opening of the prison to them that are bound, to comfort all that mourn; to give unto them beauty for ashes, the oil of joy for mourning, the garment of praise for the spirit of heaviness that they might be called trees of righteousness, the planting of the Lord.

Isaiah 61.1,3. A.V.

Who shall

separate us from the love of Christ? Shall tribulation or distress or persecution, or famine or nakedness, or peril or sword? Nay, in all these things we are more than conquerors through Him that loved us.

For I am persuaded that neither death nor life, nor angels nor principalities, nor things present nor things to come, nor height, nor depth, nor any other creature shall be able to separate us from the love of God which is in Christ Jesus.

Romans 8.35, 37-38. A.V.

THE LORD IS NEAR.

HAVE NO ANXIETY

But in everything make your requests known to God in prayer and petition with thanksgiving. Then the peace of God which is beyond our utmost understanding will keep guard over your hearts and your thoughts in Christ Jesus. All that is true, all that is noble, all that is just and pure, all that is lovable and gracious, whatever is excellent and admirable, fill all your thoughts with these.

Philippians 4.6-8. N.E.B.

OW OUR LORD JESUS CHRIST HIMSELF, AND GOD

Even our Father, which hath loved us and hath given us everlasting consolation and good hope through grace, comfort your hearts, and stablish you in every good word and work.

And the Lord direct your hearts into the love of God, and into the patient waiting for Christ.

2 Thessalonians 2.16-17; 3.5. A.V

92

LORD, YOUR DECREES ARE JUST

And even in chastening you keep faith with me.

Let your love comfort me as you have promised me. Extend your compassion to me that I may live, for your law is my delight. I shall meditate on your precepts.

Let me give my whole heart to your statutes so that I am not put to shame.

I long with all my heart for your deliverance. I have put my hope in your word.

I do not forget your statutes.

Psalm 119. 75-78, 80-81, 83. R.E.B.

THE LORD
IS MY
SHEPHERD.
I SHALL NOT
WANT.

He maketh me to lie down
    In green pastures
He leadeth me
    Beside the still waters
He restoreth my soul.

He leadeth me

In the paths of righteousness
  For His names sake.
Yea, though I walk through the valley
  Of the shadow of death
I will fear no evil
  For Thou art with me,
Thy rod and Thy staff
  They comfort me.
Thou preparest a table before me
  In the presence of mine enemies.
Thou anointest my head with oil,
  My cup runneth over.
Surely goodness and mercy shall follow me
  All the days of my life,
And I will dwell
  In the House of the Lord for ever.

Psalm 23. 1-6. A.V.

Springs
of
Fellowship

Then they that feared the Lord spake often

One to another; and the Lord hearkened and heard it. and a book of remembrance was written before Him for them that feared the Lord, and that thought upon His name.

And they shall be Mine, saith the Lord of Hosts, in that day when I make up My jewels.

Malachi 3.16-17. A.V.

The Key note of your conversation

Should not be nastiness or silliness or flippancy, but a sense of all we owe to God. Live your lives in love, the same sort of love that Christ gives us and which He perfectly expressed when He gave Himself up for us in sacrifice to God. Be filled with the Spirit, addressing one another in psalms and hymns and spiritual songs, singing and making melody to the Lord with all your heart, always giving thanks in the name of our Lord Jesus.

Ephesians 5.4, 2 J.B.P. 5.19. R.S.V.

ABIDE IN Me AND I IN you.

As the branch cannot bear fruit by itself unless it abides in the vine, neither can you except you abide in Me.
I am the vine, you are the branches. He who abides in Me and I in him, he it is who bears much fruit, for apart from Me you can do nothing.
If you abide in Me and My words abide in you, ask whatever you will and it shall be done for you.

John 15. 4-5, 7. R.S.V.

GOD WHO HAS CALLED YOU INTO FELLOWSHIP

With His Son Jesus Christ our Lord, is faithful.

I appeal to you in the name of our Lord Jesus Christ, that all of you agree with one another, so that there may be no divisions among you and that you may be perfectly united in mind and thought. Make every effort to keep the unity of the Spirit through the bond of peace.

1 Corinthians 1.9-10. N.I.V.

Ephesians 4.3. N.I.V.

IF YOU HAVE ANY ENCOURAGEMENT

From being united with Christ, if any comfort from His love, if any fellowship with the Spirit, if any tenderness and compassion, then make my joy complete by being like-minded, having the same love, being one in spirit and purpose. Do nothing out of selfish ambition or vain conceit, but in humility consider others better than yourselves.

Each of you should look not only to your own interests, but also to the interests of others.

Philippians 2.1-4. N.I.V.

How
GOOD AND
HOW PLEASANT

It is to live together as brothers in unity!
It is like fragrant oil poured on the head
And falling over the beard, Aaron's beard
When the oil runs down
Over the collar of his vestments.
It is as if the dew of Hermon were falling
On the mountains of Zion
There the Lord bestows His blessing
Life for evermore.
With deep roots and firm foundations
may you be strong to grasp Christ's love.

Psalm 133. 1-3.   R.E.B.
Ephesians 3. 18.   R.E.B.

THEY MET CONSTANTLY TO HEAR THE

Apostles teach, and to share the common life, to break bread, and to pray. A sense of awe was everywhere, and many marvels and signs were brought about through the apostles. All whose faith had drawn them together held everything in common, they would sell their property and make a general distribution. With one mind they kept up their daily attendance at the temple and breaking bread in private houses, shared their meals with unaffected joy.

Acts 2.42-47. N.E.B.

BE HUMBLE, ALWAYS AND GENTLE

And patient too. Be forbearing with one another and charitable. Spare no effort to make fast with bonds of peace the unity which the Spirit gives. There is one body and one Spirit, as there is also one hope held out in God's call to you; one Lord, one faith, one baptism; one God and Father of all, who is over all and through all and in all. Now vast the resoures of His power open to us who trust in Him.

Ephesians 4. 2-6; 1. 19. N.E.B.

THE LORD WOULD SPEAK WITH MOSES

Face to face, just as a man speaks with a friend. There is someone in Heaven to stand up for me and take my side. I want someone to plead with God for me as a man pleads for his friend. But I know there is someone in Heaven who will come at last to my defence. I will see God. I will see Him with my own eyes. We have an advocate with the Father, Jesus Christ, the righteous.

Ex.33.11; Job.16.19-21; 19.25-27. G.N.B. 1 John 2.1. A.V.

THANK GOD the FATHER OF OUR LORD

Jesus Christ, that He is our Father and the source of all mercy and comfort. For He gives us comfort in our trials so that we in turn may be able to give the same sort of strong sympathy in theirs. The more we share Christ's suffering, the more we are able to give of His encouragement. If we experience trouble we can pass on to you comfort and spiritual help; for if we ourselves have been comforted, we know how to encourage you.

2 Corinthians 1.3-7. J.B.P.

THAT I MAY KNOW HIM

AND THE POWER

Of His resurrection, and the fellowship of His sufferings, being made conformable unto His death; if by any means I might attain to the resurrection of the dead. Not as though I had already attained, either were already perfect, but this one thing I do, forgetting those things which are behind and reaching forth unto those things which are before, I press toward the mark of the high calling of God in Christ Jesus.

Philippians 3.10-14. A.V.

AT THAT TIME YOU WERE FOREIGNERS

And did not belong to God's chosen people. You had no part in the covenants which were based on God's promises to his people, and you lived in this world without hope and without God. But now, in union with Christ Jesus, you who used to be far away have been brought near by the sacrificial death of Christ. You too are built upon the foundation laid by the apostles and prophets, the corner stone being Christ Jesus himself.

Ephesians 2.12-13; 20. G.N.B.

To you whom I love, I say

Let us go on loving one another, for love comes from God. To us, the greatest demonstration of God's love for us has been His sending His only Son into the world to give us life through Him. We see real love, not in the fact that we loved God, but that He loved us and sent His Son to make personal atonement for our sins. If God loved us as much as that, surely we in our turn should love one another.

1 John 4. 7-10. J.B.P.

THAT which we have seen and heard we proclaim also to you, so that you may have fellowship with us; and our fellowship is with the Father and with His Son Jesus Christ. God is light and in Him is no darkness at all. If we say we have fellowship with Him while we walk in darkness, we lie and do not live according to the truth; but if we walk in the light, as He is in the light, we have fellowship one with another, and the blood of Jesus His Son, cleanses us from all sin.

1 John 1.3; 5-7. R.S.V.

Springs of Encouragement

I KNOW THE PLANS I HAVE FOR YOU

Declares the Lord, plans to prosper you and not to harm you, plans to give you hope and a future.

Then you will call upon Me and come and pray to Me and I will listen to you.

You will seek Me and find Me when you seek Me with all your heart.

I will be found by you, declares the Lord. Seek the Lord while He may be found.

Jeremiah 29. 11-14. N.I.V.

THE LORD DID WHAT HE HAD PROMISED.

Trust Him at all times; pour out your heart before Him.
There failed not ought of any good thing which the Lord had spoken, all came to pass.
He is faithful that promised. Has He said and shall He not do it? Or has He spoken and shall He not make it good?
The word of our God shall stand for ever. Gen. 21. 1. Ps 62.8. N.I.V. Josh. 21.45. Heb. 10.23. Num. 23.19. Is. 40.8. A.V.

I WILL NEVER LEAVE YOU NOR Forsake you. Be strong and courageous. Do not let this Book of the Law depart from your mouth, meditate on it day and night, so that you may be careful to do everything written in it. Then you will be prosperous and successful. Have not I commanded you, be strong and courageous. Do not be terrified; do not be discouraged, for the Lord your God will be with you.

Joshua 1.5-8. N.I.V.

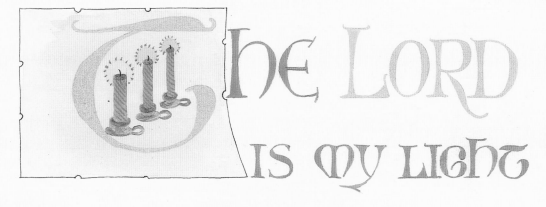

THE LORD
IS MY LIGHT
AND MY SALVATION,

Whom shall I fear? The Lord is the strength of my life, of whom shall I be afraid? In the time of trouble He shall hide me in His pavilion, in the secret of His tabernacle shall He hide me. Thou hast been my help, leave me not, neither forsake me, oh God of my salvation. Teach me Thy way oh Lord and lead me in a plain path. Wait on the Lord, be of good courage, and He shall strength-en thine heart. Psalm 27. 1, 5, 9, 11, 14. A.V.

The Lord is my
ROCK, MY FORTRESS

And my deliverer, in whom I take refuge.
He is my shield and my stronghold. I
call to the Lord who is worthy of praise
In my distress I called to the Lord. He
heard my voice; my cry came before Him.
The Lord was my support. He brought
me out into a spacious place; He rescued
me because He delighted in me.
Therefore I will praise you oh Lord.
I will sing praises to your name.

Psalm 18. 2, 3, 6, 16, 19, 49. N.I.V.

Fear thou not for I am with thee

Be not dismayed for I am thy God, I will strengthen thee, yea I will help thee; yea I will uphold thee with the right hand of My righteousness. Behold, all they that were incensed against thee shall be ashamed and confounded; they shall be as nothing, and they that strive with you shall perish. For I the Lord your God will hold your right hand saying unto thee, Fear not, I will help thee.   Isaiah 41. 10, 11, 13. A.V.

FEAR NOT FOR I HAVE REDEEMED THEE.

I have called thee by thy name; thou art mine. When thou passest through the waters, I will be with thee, and through the rivers, they shall not overflow thee; when thou walkest through the fire, thou shalt not be burned, neither shall the flame kindle upon thee.
Since thou wast precious in My sight thou hast been honourable and I have loved thee.
Fear not for I am with thee.

Isaiah 43. 1, 2, 4, 5. A.V

Though I Walk in the Midst of Trouble

You preserve my life, you stretch out your hand against the anger of my foes, with your right hand you save me. The Lord will fulfil His purpose for me. Because you are my help, I sing in the shadow of your wings.

How great is your goodness which you have stored up for those who fear you. Be strong and take heart, all you who hope in the Lord.

Psalm 138.7; 63.7; 31. 19-34. N.I.V.

HAST THOU

NOT KNOWN, HAST THOU NOT HEARD

That the everlasting God, the Creator of the ends of the earth, fainteth not, neither is weary? There is no searching of His understanding. He giveth power to the faint; and to them that have no might, He increaseth strength. Even the youths shall faint and be weary and the young men shall utterly fall, but they that wait upon the Lord shall renew their strength; they shall mount up with wings like eagles; they shall run and not be weary; and they shall walk and not faint.

Isaiah 40. 28-31. A.V.

Though
THE FIG TREE

DOES NOT BUD,

And there are no grapes on the vines,
Though the olive crop fails
And the fields produce no food,
Though there are no sheep in the pen
And no cattle in the stalls,
Yet I will rejoice in the Lord,
I will be joyful in God, my Saviour
The sovereign Lord is my strength
He makes my feet like the feet of a deer,
He enables me to go on the heights.

Habakkuk 3. 17-19. N.I.V.

WE ARE HANDICAPPED ON ALL SIDES

But we are never frustrated; we are puzzled but never in despair. We are persecuted, but we never have to stand it alone; we may be knocked down but we are never knocked out. Every day we experience something of the death of Jesus, so that we may also know the power of the life of Jesus. Yes, we are always being exposed to death for Jesus' sake, so that the life of Jesus may be plainly seen in our mortal lives. 2 Corinthians 4.8-10. J.B.P.

Let us draw near to God with a sincere heart in full assurance of faith. Let us consider how we may spur one another on towards love and good deeds. Let us encourage one another.

Do not throw away your confidence, it will be richly rewarded.

You need to persevere so that when you have done the will of God, you will receive what He has promised.

Hebrews 10. 22, 24, 25, 35. N.I.V.

I AM NOT SAYING THIS BECAUSE

I am in need, for I have learned to be content whatever the circumstances. I know what it is to be in need and know what it is to have plenty. I have learned the secret of being content in any and every situation, whether well fed or hungry, whether living in plenty or in want. I can do everything through Him who gives me strength. The exceeding greatness of His power to usward who believe.

Philippians 4.11-13 N.I.V.

PRAISED BE THE GOD AND FATHER

Of our Lord Jesus Christ! In His great mercy by the resurrection of Jesus Christ from the dead. He gave us new birth into a living hope, the hope of an inheritance, reserved in heaven for you, which nothing can destroy or spoil or wither. Because you put your faith in God, you are under the protection of His power until the salvation now in readiness is revealed at the end of time. This is cause for great joy.

1 Peter 1.3-5. R.E.B.

Springs
of
Hope

In this you
GREATLY REJOICE,
Though now for a little while you may have
to suffer grief in all kinds of trials. These
have come so that your faith, of greater
worth than gold, may be proved genuine
and may result in praise, glory and honour
when Jesus Christ is revealed. Though
you have not seen Him, you love Him and
even though you do not see Him now, you
believe in Him and are filled with an
inexpressible and glorious joy, the goal of
your faith, the salvation of your souls.

1 Peter 1.6-9. N.I.V.

127

IN ALL OUR PRAYERS TO GOD

We thank Him for you, because we have heard of the faith you hold in Christ Jesus and the love you bear towards all God's people. Both spring from the hope stored up for you in heaven, that hope of which you learned when the message of the true gospel first came to you. In the same way it is coming to men the whole world over; everywhere it is growing and bearing fruit as it does among you.

Colossians 1.3-6. N.E.B.

Be Ready At Any

Time To Give A

Quiet and reverent answer to any man who wants a reason for the hope that you have within you. Make sure that your conscience is perfectly clear, so that if men should speak slanderously of you as rogues they may come to feel ashamed of themselves for libelling your good Christian behaviour.

If it is the will of God that you should suffer, it is really better to suffer unjustly than because you have deserved it.

1 Peter 3.15-17. J.B.P.

The TRUTH IS CHRIST

WAS RAISED TO LIFE

The firstfruits of the harvest of the dead. As in Adam all die, so in Christ all will be brought to life, Christ the first fruits, and afterwards at His coming, those who belong to Christ. Then comes the end, when He delivers up the kingdom to God the Father, after deposing every sovereignty, authority and power. For He is destined to reign until God has put all enemies under His feet, and the last enemy to be deposed is death.

1 Corinthians 15. 20-26. R.E.B.

THE GRACE OF GOD HAS DAWNED UPON

The world with healing for all mankind; and by it we are disciplined to renounce godless ways and worldly desires, and to live a life of temperance, honesty and godliness in the present age, looking forward to the happy fulfilment of our hopes when the splendour of our great God and Saviour will appear. He it is who sacrificed Himself for us, to set us free from all wickedness and to make us a pure people marked out for His own.

Titus 2.11-14. N.E.B.

WE ARE CITIZENS OF HEAVEN,

Our outlook goes beyond this world to the hopeful expectation of the Saviour who will come from Heaven, the Lord Jesus Christ. He will change these wretched bodies of ours so that they resemble His own glorious body, by that power of His which makes Him the master of everything that is.

So, my brothers whom I love and long for, my joy and my crown, do stand firmly in the Lord.

Philippians 3.20-21; 4.1. J.B.P.

I CONSIDER THAT OUR PRESENT SUFFERINGS Are not worth comparing with the glory that will be revealed in us. The creation itself will be liberated from its bondage to decay and brought into the glorious freedom of the children of God. For in this hope we were saved. But hope that is seen is no hope at all. Who hopes for what he already has? But if we hope for what we do not yet have, we wait for it patiently. In the same way the Spirit helps us.

Romans 8. 18-21; 24-26. N.I.V.

KEEP THE FIRES OF THE SPIRIT BURNING

As we do our work for the Lord; base your happiness on your hope in Christ. When trials come endure them patiently: steadfastly maintain the habit of prayer. Give freely to fellow Christians in want, never grudging a meal or a bed to those who need them.

And as for those who try to make your life a misery, bless them.

As far as your responsibility goes, live at peace with everyone. Romans 12. 12-16. J.B.P.

137

WE WANT EACH OF YOU TO SHOW

This same diligence to the very end, in order to make your hope sure. God did this so that, by two unchangeable things in which it is impossible for God to lie, we who have fled to take hold of the hope offered to us may be greatly encouraged. We have this hope as an anchor for the soul, firm and secure. It enters the inner sanctuary behind the curtain, where Jesus, who went before us, has entered on our behalf.   Hebrews 6.11-20. N.I.V.

MAY GOD,
THE SOURCE
OF ALL PERSEVERANCE

And all encouragement, grant that you may agree with one another after the manner of Christ Jesus, and so with one mind and one voice may praise God. In a word, accept one another as Christ accepted us, to the glory of God. And may God, who is the ground of hope, fill you with all joy and peace as you lead the life of faith, until by the power of the Holy Spirit you overflow with hope.   Romans 15.5-7, 13. R.E.B.

THE FAITH OF GOD'S ELECT AND THE

Knowledge of the truth that leads to godliness, a faith and knowledge resting on the hope of eternal life which God, who does not lie, promised before the beginning of time, and at His appointed season, He brought His word to light so that having been justified by His grace we might become heirs having the hope of eternal life. This is a trustworthy saying and I want you to stress these things.

Titus 1.1-2; 3.7 N.I.V.

140

Now great is the love the Father

Has lavished on us, that we should be called children of God! And that is what we are! The reason the world does not know us is that it did not know Him. What we will be has not yet been made known. But we know that when He appears, we shall be like Him, for we shall see Him as He is.
Everyone who has this hope in Him purifies himself, just as He is pure.

1 John 3. 1-3. N.I.V.

THEREFORE ARE THEY BEFORE THE THRONE

Of God, and serve Him day and night in His temple. They shall hunger no more, neither thirst any more; neither shall the sun light on them, nor any heat. For the Lamb which is in the midst of the throne shall feed them, and shall lead them into living fountains of waters: and God shall wipe away all tears from their eyes.

These were redeemed from among men; they are without fault before the throne of God.

Revelation 7. 15-17: 14. 4-5. N.I.V.

BECAUSE GOD WANTED TO MAKE THE

Unchanging nature of His purpose very clear, He confirmed it with an oath. God did this so that, by two unchangeable things in which it is impossible for God to lie, we who have fled to take hold of the hope offered to us may be greatly encouraged. We have this hope as an anchor for the soul, firm and secure. It enters the inner sanctuary behind the curtain, where Jesus, who went before us, has entered on our behalf, a High Priest for ever.

Hebrews 6. 17-20. N.I.V.

LORD, grant that we may be
diligent to read Thy Word
wherein is Wisdom, wherein
is the Royal Law, wherein
are the lively Oracles of God,
and that reading it we may
daily increase in the knowledge of Thyself and love and
serve Thee with more perfect
heart.

Source unknown.

Abbreviations for Translations

A.V.	Authorised Version or
	King James Version
G.N.B.	Good News Bible
J.B.P.	J.B.Phillips
J.M.	James Moffatt
N.E.B.	New English Bible
N.I.V.	New International Version
R.E.B.	Revised English Bible
R.S.V.	Revised Standard Version

Index

Book	Reference	Version	Page	Book	Reference	Version	Page
Genesis	21.1.	N.I.V	115	Proverbs	4.1; 20-23	R.S.V	2
Exodus	33. 11.	G.N.B.	106	Isaiah	9. 6-7.	A.V.	58
Numbers	6. 24-26	N.I.V	51		11. 6-9	A.V.	56
	23. 10.	A.V.	115		12. 2-5	A.V.	54
Deuteronomy	21. 24.	A.V.	115		25. 1-4; 9.	A.V.	154
	32. 2-4, 6.	N.I.V.	147.		29. 19	A.V.	52
Joshua	1. 5-8	N.I.V.	116		30. 15; 18-19	A.V.	55
	21. 45.	A.V.	115		32. 15-18	G.N.B	52
Job	16. 19-21; 19. 25-27	G.N.B.	106		40. 1; 11-14.	A.V.	82
Psalm	4. 6-8.	N.I.V	67		40. 8	A.V.	115
	5. 2-3, 11.	G.N.B.	51		41. 10-11; 13	A.V.	119
	16. 11.	A.V.	50		40. 28-31	A.V.	122
	16. 19-21	G.N.B.	122		43. 1-2; 4-5	A.V.	120
	9. 1-2.	G.N.B.	51		48. 17-18; 21-22	N.I.V.	59
	18. 2,3, 6, 16, 19				51. 11-13; 16	A.V.	86
	49.	N.I.V.	118		52. 7; 10-12	N.I.V	54
	19. 25-27	G.N.B.	106		54. 8, 7; 10-12	A.V.	85
	23. 1-6.	A.V.	94-95		54. 10, 13, 17.	N.I.V.	55
	27. 1,5,9,11,14.	A.V.	117		55. 11-12	A.V.	55
	30. 5.	A.V.	53		55. 12-15	A.V.	53
	31. 19-34	N.I.V.	121		61. 1-3	A.V.	89
	34. 1-18.	N.I.V.	67		63. 7-9	A.V.	37
	43. 3-4.	A.V.	50		65. 14, 19, 24	A.V.	56
	47. 2-4, 6-9	N.I.V.	75	Jeremiah	17. 17-18	N.I.V.	18
	51. 1-2, 7-8, 10-12	A.V.	53		29. 11-14	N.I.V.	114
	61. 11.	A.V.	50		31. 3.	N.I.V.	35
	62. 5-12	N.I.V.	56	Habakkuk	3. 17-19	N.I.V.	123
	62. 8.	N.I.V.	115		3. 18-19	R.E.B.	57
	63. 1-8	N.I.V.	68	Zephaniah	3. 17-20	R.E.B	57
	63. 7.	N.I.V.	121	Malachi	3. 16-17	A.V.	98
	66. 18-20	N.I.V.	86	Matthew	7. 16.	N.E.B.	14
	66. 1-20	N.I.V.	74		11, 28-30	A.V.	60
	71. 14, 19-23	N.I.V.	72	Mark	11. 22-24	N.I.V.	10
	73. 24-25	A.V.	50	Luke	11. 10	N.I.V.	31
	85. 10.	A.V.	67		12. 27-28, 31	J.B.P.	20
	91. 1-2, 14, 16	A.V.	57		14. 27, 16, 33	N.E.B.	77
	91. 1,9-11; 14-16	N.I.V.	36		15. 4-5; 7	R.S.V.	116
	103. 1-5, 22.	A.V.	76	John	1. 10-14	N.E.B	4
	103. 4	A.V.	52		3. 16-18	N.I.V.	9
	104. 33-34	A.V.	52		3. 36	A.V.	3
	119. 75-78; 80-81,83	R.E.B	93		4. 11-14	N.I.V.	14
	119. 89	A.V.	55		5. 24	N.I.V.	12
	119. 165	N.I.V.	50		5. 39-40	N.I.V.	13
	133. 1-3	R.E.B.	103		7. 38-39	N.I.V.	13
	138. 7.	N.I.V.	121		10. 10-11; 27-30	R.S.V	6
	145. 1,3,5,13,18,21	N.I.V.	69		11. 25	N.I.V.	12
	146. 5.	A.V	52		14. 6	A.V.	3
	147. 1,3,5,7,11, 20	N.I.V	91		14. 11-14	N.I.V.	14
	150. 1-6.	N.I.V.	66		14. 27, 1	N.E.B.	61

Index

Book	Reference	Version	Page	Book	Reference	Version	Page
John	15. 4-5, 7	R.S.V.	100	Philippians	4.4	A.V.	43
	15. 13.	N.I.V.	50		4. 6-7	A.V	62
	15. 8-15	N.E.B.	38		4. 6-8	N.E.B.	91
	15. 13-17	N.E.B.	30		4. 11-13.	N.I.V.	126
	16. 22-24	R.E.B.	61		4. 13-19	N.I.V.	143
	16. 31-33	NE.B.	61	Colossians	1. 3.-6	N.E.B.	131
	17. 1-3	N.I.V	7		2. 7.	J.B.P.	58
Acts	2. 42-47	N.E.B.	104		3. 15	A.V.	78
	4.12.	A.V.	12		3. 15-17	N.I.V.	63
Romans	3. 23-26	N.I.V.	11	2 Thessalonians	2. 16-17; 3.5.	A.V.	92
	5. 1-5	N.I.V.	21		3. 16.	A.V.	78
	6. 20-23	N.E.B.	10	Titus	1. 1-2, 3-7	N.I.V	140
	8.6.	A.V.	52		2. 11-14	N.E.B.	134
	8. 18, 21, 24-26	N.I.V.	136		3. 5-8	N.E.B.	8
	8. 35, 37-39	N.I.V.	45	Hebrews	4. 14-16	R.S.V	84
	8. 35; 37-38	A.V.	90		6. 11-20	N.I.V.	138
	10. 17, 13-15	A.V.	23		10. 22-35	N.I.V.	125
	11. 33-36	N.I.V.	95		6. 17-20	N.I.V	143
	12. 9-13	G.N.B.	42		10. 21-23	G.N.B.	25
	12. 12-16	J.B.P.	137		10. 23	A.V.	115
	15. 13	N.I.V.	66		11. 1; 5-6	N.I.V	26
	15. 5-7, 13	R.E.B.	139		12. 2	G.N.B	27
	15. 4-7	J.B.P.	87		13. 15, 20	N.I.V	77
1 Corinthians	1. 9-10	N.I.V.	117	James	5. 14-16	N.I.V.	28
	2. 2-5	N.I.V.	22	1 Peter	1. 3-5	R.E.B.	130
	7. 15	A.V.	52		1. 4-7	N.I.V.	30
	13. 1-13	J.M	46-47		1. 6-9	N.E.B.	29
	15. 20-26	R.E.B.	133		1. 6-9	N.I.V.	126
2 Corinthians	1. 3.-7	N.I.V.	88		2. 9-12	N.I.V.	73
	1. 3.-7	J.B.P.	107		2. 24	A.V.	27
	4. 8-10	J.B.P	124		3. 15-17	J.B.P	132
	5. 21	A.V.	27		4. 12-14	A.V.	60
	6. 10	J.B.P	58		5. 6-10	R.S.V	83
Galatians	5. 22	J.B.P	58	1 John	1. 3, 5, 7	R.S.V	111
Ephesians	1. 3-6	N.I.V.	70		2. 1	A.V.	106
	1. 19	N.E.B.	121		3. 1	N.I.V	35
	2. 12-13, 20	G.N.B	109		3. 1-3	N.I.V	141
	2. 8-13	G.N.B	24		3. 11-13, 20	R.S.V	5
	3. 16-19	N.I.V	44		3. 13-16	N.E.B.	41
	3. 18	R.E.B.	103		4. 7.	G.N.B.	34
	4. 3.	N.I.V.	101		4. 7-10	J.B.P.	110
	4. 2-6	N.E.B.	105		4. 16-21	N.E.B.	40
	5. 4, 2.	J.B.P	99		5. 4, 14	N.I.V.	31
	5. 19	R.S.V.	115		5. 11-13, 20	R.S.V	5
Philippians	1. 9; 2. 1-2	R.E.B.	43	Jude	24	A.V	48
	2. 1-4	N.I.V.	102	Revelation	2. 1-6	N.I.V	14
	2. 2.	A.V.	43		5. 11-14	R.E.B.	78
	2. 5-11	A.V	47		7. 15-17	A.V	142
	3. 10-14	A.V.	108		14. 4-5	N.I.V	142
	3. 20-21	J.B.P	135		22. 1-5	NEB.	15

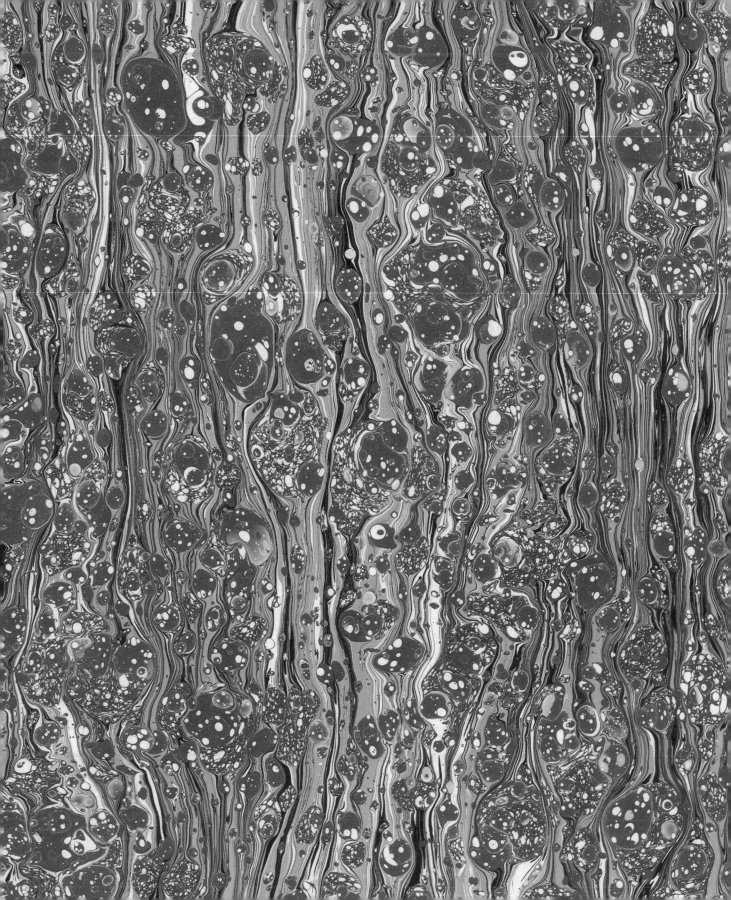